The Fall of the American Empire
By Mark Wrobel

Cover Created & Designed by Jazzy Kitty Publications
Logo Designs by Andre M. Saunders/Jess Zimmerman
Editor: Anelda Lukesia Attaway

© 2021 Mark Wrobel
ISBN 978-1-954425-35-4
Library of Congress Control Number: 2021922902

All rights reserved. This book is protected by the copyright laws of the United States of America. This book may not be copied or reprinted for commercial gain or profit. The use of short quotations or occasional page copying for personal or group study is permitted and encouraged. Permission will be granted upon request. This book is for Worldwide Distribution and printed in the United States of America, published by Jazzy Kitty Publications utilizing Microsoft Publishing Software.

ACKNOWLEDGMENT

First and foremost, I acknowledge God and thank Him for sustaining me through life with my disability. Also, my father, Roman Wrobel because he was my rock and my pillar.

DEDICATION

I dedicate this book to my dear friend Rosemarie Arcaro and her father, Charles P. Arcaro.
I appreciate your support!

TABLE OF CONTENTS

INTRODUCTION i
CHAPTER 1 – Liberalism is a Mental Disorder 01
CHAPTER 2 – Is the Economy Stupid? 04
CHAPTER 3 – Victory for the Terrorist 08
CHAPTER 4 – American Education System Has Gone to the Dogs 11
CHAPTER 5 – The Moral Degradation of America 15
CHAPTER 6 – Can the United States of America Be Saved? 18
CHAPTER 7 – Replacement of the Population in the United States 23
CHAPTER 8 – The Thin Blue Line 28
CHAPTER 9 – The Incompetence of the American Senior Citizen 33
CHAPTER 10 – The Existence of a Nation 37
ABOUT THE AUTHOR 41
REFERENCES 43

INTRODUCTION

I wasn't going to write another political book. However, the situation in the United States has dramatically changed, and may I say that it has not changed for the better. The situation has gotten worse on all fronts.

By writing this book, I hope to give my final warning about what is coming in this country. Because let's face it, we, the American people, don't have a place to go. So, I hope when you read this book, you can prepare yourself physically and spiritually for what things may come here in the United States.

CHAPTER 1

Liberalism is a Mental Disorder

You've got to love the liberal left and the Israel firsters here in America. That is because the liberals say that the conservatives are not tolerant enough and the Israel firsters say Israel has the right to exist.

Let us examine both of these issues for a moment.

Israel firsters say that Israel has a right to exist. In this case, I disagree with this particular statement because no country has a right to exist. Countries exist around the world because they are strong economically, morally, intellectually, and militarily.

What do you mean by that? Well, I will be more than happy to explain it to you. Let us look at the economic aspects of the United States as of this writing. We have a lot of people on some sort of government benefit/assistance. Of course, some people may say that this is because of the pandemic we are experiencing right now. They would not be wrong in this case. Nevertheless, you must understand that this welfare system was not designed to handle this type of situation. So, in this case, the welfare system will eventually collapse on itself.

The second issue that we will be discussing is moral issues. When you have our government pushing the issue of transgender on the American people, then we will have to say liberalism is a mental disorder. Our liberal politicians say that we, the American people have to accept the transversal. I say, in this case, absolutely not. This issue has come up in our US military, where the liberal left and their communist brethren are pushing the issue of transgender people. In my opinion, basically to destroy one of the strongest militaries/security apparatus within.

One of the famous Roman orators by the name of Marcus Tullius Cicero said, "A nation can survive its fools and even the ambitious. But it cannot survive treason from within. An enemy at the gates is less formidable, for he is known and carries his banner openly."

I have a question in this case, what is this Roman gentleman speaking about? I think the issues of what is happening to our nation right now? Look, some of you might be asking a question right about now, are you the moral police of the United States? Absolutely not, but when our government pushes and promotes destructive behavior on our most sacred institution like the United States military, I will definitely say something about that.

I know that some of you might find these transgender issues funny. However, let's look at this scenario from the other point of view. This will definitely affect you guys, who like to hang out with the ladies of the night. If you get my meaning, say what if you try to pick up a lady of the night and they turned out to be a man? What would you do? You see, this type of behavior not only has the possibility of being destructive, not only on our security apparatus of this nation. However, I know that this scenario that I gave about the ladies of the night might be funny, but I want you to see how this disgusting transgender behavior has the potential to affect have a negative effect on our own social lives.

The last issue that will be addressed in this book will be the intellectual issue. What is that mean? It just means that there is no education in the education department. So, in this case, there is no education in our schools.

If you don't understand anything about these issues mentioned in this chapter, do not worry; I will break those issues down in upcoming chapters and make them easier to understand.

For now, all you have to understand when discussing an intellectual issue in this particular chapter, that our schools have become nothing more but the communist Bolsheviks' indoctrination centers for the next generation of the communist bombs. Schools no longer fulfill their responsibility of educating and preparing our children for the real world, whether you go to grade school, high school, or even college.

CHAPTER 2

Is the Economy Stupid?

The United States of America was once the world's economic power and the whole world was proud too. People have tried to imitate the United States economic system, sometimes with great success, sometimes not. I think those days are behind us.

There are many reasons for this state of affairs here in the United States and around the world. One of the reasons that our economy is not doing so well is because of quantitative easing. What does that mean, you may ask? Well, the actual definition of quantitative easing is below: (https://www.investopedia.com/terms/q/quantitative-easing.asp,2020).
What this actually means in reality, that the central banks and the Federal Reserve are actually printing money from thin air. That is because there might not be any gold in Fort Knox to actually back the dollar. Let's be honest, there has been no gold in Fort Knox since the 1970s. That is because in the 1970s, Richard E. Nixon, the President of the United States at that time, took us off the gold standard. (2020). Since then, our economic problems have doubled or tripled. Nowadays, what you have added into the mix is inflation. Let me give you an example of what I'm talking about.

For example, a bottle of Diet Coke in the dollar store costs about $1.10. However, when you add inflation into the mix, the price of Diet Coke now is about $2.20. Because of inflation and later on, this possibly may turn into hyperinflation. We will not know what the price of goods and services will cost us from one day to the next. With the printing of money out of thin air plus inflation, we as a nation are headed for a major economic disaster.

Another issue might be causing us another economic problem down the road: the shortage of materials to produce the goods we need to buy.

Let me give you an example of what I'm talking about.

Not too long ago, you could have bought a nice Ford F1 50 used for about $18,000. However, because today's cars mostly have computers in them and they are basically computers on wheels. Because of the shortage of materials to make those computer chips for those cars that we depend on every day for transportation needs, the price will definitely skyrocket. When that happens, when the transportation of goods and services goes up. You will definitely be paying more for common household items, such as groceries and other things you will definitely pay more to obtain them. Many economists say that this is unsustainable. May I say they are absolutely correct.

The next question should be who is and why are they doing this?

Well, those of you who have read my previous books already know the answer to that particular question. However, I will be more than happy to answer this question for those of you who do not know.

You have to understand that most decisions made by our politicians are no longer being made in our capitals. Even worse, those decisions that affect us in our so-called daily lives are not even made by our senators and our congressmen. Now days even the President of the United States does not make decisions on their own. However, those decisions that affect us are made by organizations such as the Builder Burg Group and many others, which embrace one-world government and want us to be slaves to them.

The next world power will be China and Russia. That is because those two countries, after the fall of Afghanistan, control the precious metals market. Because, let's face it, that war that we have just lost, by the way, it was not about women's rights in Afghanistan. It was definitely not about some terrorist in the cave by the name of Osama bin Laden. However, it was all about precious; precious metals.

As you all know, the most wealth of nickel, gold, and other precious metals are located in Afghanistan. We will get into what this means for an average US citizen in the next couple of chapters. I'm going to tell you that whoever has control over precious metals and where the precious metals can be extracted from that particular country or country will be very rich and definitely become the next superpower.

In the not-too-distant future, the United States dollar will lose its power as the world reserve currency. That is when the collapse of the US dollar will begin. This will definitely happen in the not-too-distant future here in the United States. Let's face it the US dollar itself is not being backed by gold. What is that mean, you may ask? This means that our dollar is not backed by anything except by faith that there is gold in Fort Knox and the Federal Reserve bank. However, this faith may be misplaced.

I know what you are thinking right about now. What will happen if the US dollar all of a sudden stops being the world's reserve currency? Well, the answer to that question is very bleak. Our inflation will turn into hyperinflation. Then we will be in real trouble because we will not know the prices of common goods and services from one day to the next. Things like cars and other durable goods will be more expensive. Because of the chip shortage for your computers that run our cars are made from the precious metals mentioned above. So, in this case, I'm going to tell you that we are headed for a major economic disaster in the short term.

CHAPTER 3

Victory for the Terrorist

Ladies and gentlemen, unfortunately, I have some bad news. America's loss of the war in Afghanistan is the biggest victory for terrorists and other totalitarian regimes like Russia, China, and North Korea.

You all remember the words of President George W. Bush after September 11, "either you are with the terrorist or with us."

Well, I am not in support of any terrorist, or I am not promoting anti-Americanism. In this particular book, all I want to do is give you a good analytical point to do your best and prepare yourself for the total economic collapse that will happen shortly, not just in the United States but all over the world. I am sorry that some of you cannot think for yourself, take the situation and analyze it, and make appropriate preparations for what is coming to the United States and what will happen in the world because of the biggest blunder in the military history of the United States.

I know what you're next question is going to be. Why do you say that after the fall of Afghanistan, there will be a major economic collapse in the United States and worldwide?

Well, I'm going to answer this question for you.

There was one other superpower from 1945 until 1989; this was the Empire of the Soviet Union or USSR for short. In the late 1989, you all remember that the Soviet Union had to leave Afghanistan because they knew that their empire was going bankrupt. What do you guys think happened a couple of months later after the Russians withdrew from Afghanistan in the late 1989 and early 1990. That is correct, ladies and gentlemen, the Soviet empire collapsed on itself, and it's dissolved. When the United States collapses because of the consequences of pulling out of Afghanistan. When our economy collapses, the whole world will collapse. That is because whether you want to or not, the US dollar is still the world reserve currency. However, when our economy collapses, the US dollar will become useless all over the world. We will definitely be experiencing what people in the former Soviet Union experienced after the fall of their communistic system.

I know that some of you may say that most of the good-looking Russian ladies or girls turn to prostitution to support themselves and their families. Well, I know what some of you American ladies are thinking. You're saying to yourself, *"Oh, I won't do that because this is immoral or that is not moral."* Well, when it comes to survival, a person can be very ruthless. However, I think that the American people have been robbed of their what we call survival instinct because of their weakness of the religious institutions. This is happening because of several factors, 1. Most people in America have been taught by their dear religious leaders to turn the other cheek when somebody hits them in one.

The other reason is that the fathers and mothers turn to raise their children to the state, and our men who are so-called fathers lack a backbone. However, some people in America still have some moral values, and they may survive or they may not.

I know what your next question will be, do you like the Russian or the Arab hookers? In this case, I will answer with a definite yes. That is because I may not like what they do. However, at least they have something that most Americans have lost, which is their survival instinct for themselves and their families.

This is going to be very important in our post-American economic collapse. Suppose you do not have well-rounded survival instincts. In that case, it will be virtually impossible for you to survive things that will come after the United States economic collapse. You see, after we have lost the war in Afghanistan, it is only a matter of time when the United States of America will collapse.

Of course, many people are trying to predict the economic collapse of the United States. However, this isn't easy to do. However, we can predict that this particular economic collapse will be very slow. This is very good because you still have time to make the necessary preparations for the upcoming economic collapse.

I'm here to tell you that it will be hard for you to make sense of everything after the economic collapse without your survival instincts. However, if you prepare for it now, you will have a better chance of making it for you and your family during the hard times coming to the United States.

CHAPTER 4

American Education System Has Gone to the Dogs

In this chapter, we will be discussing our lack of intellectual power because of the failure of our educational system.

Our public schools are nothing more than indoctrination centers, which our Judeo Bolsheviks run to make us slaves to the global New World Order.

From the 1950s through the 1990s, there was no anti-Americanism being taught in our public schools. Our teachers had good and honest discussions to some degree. However, from the late 90s to 2000, everything has changed in our public schools. Back in those days, the education system wasn't that great anyway. You still could find teachers who cared a little bit about their students.

When the late 90s came upon us, this all changed. For example, if you could not learn at the same pace as everyone else, your teachers placed you in special education classes. They told you that you will not going to amount to anything. Also, you'll never going to get your college degree. This was back in the good old days of the 90s, but this has gone further of the rails. Nowadays, you are taught in your dear old public school that you are bad. However, you illegal immigrant who came from a garbage can country is better than you and you should bow to him and basically worship him.

As an American, in my opinion, you should not do this, no matter what anyone else tells you. If your teacher starts to promote communist /collectivist ideas, you should tell them to go to Hell.

Those of you who have read my previous books already know who is and what is behind the collapse of our education system. Nowadays, if you show a little bit of ingenuity and think outside the box in school, your parents will be called for a parent-teacher conference. Or you might be put on is a psychiatric medication, that is because today's teachers like obedient students. But today's teachers do not like students in school that can think for themselves. Today, your schools are just prisons for your mind because today's schools are not where learning takes place. Today's education is not a place of intellectual learning but a communist and Bolshevik anti-American indoctrination center.

However, there is a way to break away from the traditional education system, which is why we have the Internet. Because of the Internet you can, practically teach yourself anything you want or need to learn. The traditional education system is obsolete nowadays; knowledge is at your fingertips. You don't have to put up with the so-called public schools. There are also alternatives such as online schools or charter schools. Whether they are right for you, you will have to do your research on this particular subject.

There is one more aspect of our education system that will be discussed in this chapter. Why are the Chinese, the Arabs and countries like Dubai and Saudi Arabia beating us in our education system versus their education system? That is because they are not a wishy-washy blah blah blah society. They do not give a one iota about the transversals or any other degeneracy. They do not spend time on BS subjects like this.

In China, these kids are taught writing, reading, and mathematics. However, they are also taught martial arts and how to make tough decisions in a crisis. Also, the Chinese and the Arabs put very hard pressure on information technology and robotics, and basically, those kids are being prepared for the future and the changing world.

The Chinese and the Arabs of our giving to their children is an instinct of survival and preservation of their nation and identity. We, the American people, are becoming too soft. If we had two go through World War II all over again, I don't think we would be able to do it with today's military and our technical know-how.

In our schools, patriotism is not being talked about when teachers remove an American flag from their classroom and sing that it is a symbol of hate. The Arab and the Chinese are laughing at us all the way to the bank.

I know what you think that you don't have tolerance; in this case, you are absolutely correct.

All, by the way, I know what America is, I know what America was, and I know what America could be. If we do not restore the self-preservation mechanism, that means the only people we should worry about is ourselves. We will not have a chance of surviving as a nation. If the American people grow some guts and put ourselves and our nation first, then we will have a chance of survival. However, for us to accomplish this, we have to restore our education system and our schools.

I know your next question: Can we, as the American people, save our nation from the coming disaster? Absolutely, however, there will have to be some drastic measures taken to save our nation.

One of those measures would have to be that the parents of the kids in America today should raise them to be just like the 300 Spartans. This means none of this, goody two shoes, wishy-washy parenting. Parents in

America should be allowed to parent and if it means that you would have to go once in a while to your child's school to see what they are being taught, then so be it.

CHAPTER 5

The Moral Degradation of America

Before we get into this type of discussion of the issue that will be discussed in this chapter. I'll tell you this much I do not care what people do behind closed doors of the bedrooms as long as it does not involve people under the age of consent. I do not care what orifice you use to get pleasure from. However, when the transgender agenda and other deviant behavior issues affect the security of our nation, our society, and our society's social morals as an American citizen with some moral compass and backbone, I will speak out about that.

Maybe you do not understand what I'm talking about, and that's okay. Please allow me to explain. There have been several legislation or legislations past that allows people with transgender tendencies to serve in the United States military. I do not agree with it because this type of behavior destroys the unit's unity and cohesion. This type of behavior has a very negative impact on the mission of the United States Armed Forces.

Even from the aesthetic point of view, can you imagine a guy who feels that he's a woman wearing a United States military dress uniform? But instead of wearing pants with the uniform, he is wearing a woman's skirt. This is a guy. I mean, think about how this disgusting this would really look. Instead of wearing dress shoes with the dress uniform, he would wear the ladies' high-heeled shoes. Can you imagine what that would look like?

Can you imagine what the people in the Muslim world, our thinking of us or about us if this were put into practice? Now that is enough about the ladies of the night, but imagine us guys going to a bar, and if you try to pick up a girl, but instead of a girl, the girl turns out to be a guy. I think this would be totally embarrassing. But not in but nowadays, who knows because American people don't have a backbone or moral compass or even some moral fortitude to say, this is right, and this is wrong.

They say in America Islam is the fastest-growing religion in America today. However, did the American people ever bother to ask why that is? That is because the Muslim people at least have some backbone and moral fortitude to say that this is right and wrong, and we will not take any of your crap from any of you, you useless communist bombs.

However, I think the moral decline of the United States will continue, especially when the parents of the children promote this transgender behavior. Those types of parents should not have children. Look, tolerance is okay. However, ultra tolerance can be and is very destructive to the existence of the nation.

Ladies and gentlemen, even tolerance has its limits. My question to you is, when are the American people going to say enough is enough? When will the American people grow a pair and start to stand up for themselves and the good old US of A for this nation?

Well, some people say that we will leave the United States if the situation gets worse. Not so fast, Johnson, other countries will not take you because other countries have stricter immigration laws than we do here in America. I will provide you with references to some of those laws in my reference section.

I know that there is no education in the education department. There is no security in the Homeland Security Department. There is no morality in the Christian religious department either.

I do not know if this nation will survive much longer in its present form? That is because the American people have lost their moral and ethical compass. Unfortunately, without any morality or ethics, the United States has no chance of survival, of things to come. If we don't teach our generation what's right and wrong and if we promote the agenda of if it feels good to do it on the road, then we as a people, not only as a nation we are finished.

CHAPTER 6

Can the United States of America Be Saved?

May I say that this is a very hard question to answer. The reason for this is that there was one man, who tried to do this, his name is Donald J Trump. There is talk that he'll try to run for president again. The question is should Donald Trump run for president?

The answer to that question is absolutely not, and here's why not, that is because I do not think that the American people themselves want America to exist, let us examine little bit closer this phenomenon, this is because every time former president Donald Trump took some drastic steps, to try to save this nation called the United States of America, everybody, from the communist Bolshevik left jumped on him like a pack of wolves.

Every time he tried to improve the US economy, the Judeo Bolshevik left, always told him to take a hike.

My question to you is how can a president do anything good for this nation when there is no support for his ideas in the Senate or any United States every time he tries to do something. The other thing is that he had to deal with the Rino Republicans and the never-Trump Republic, and so in this case, how could he as president get anything done.

In my opinion, also he was the week president that is because, when Donald J Trump said to the reporters his election was stolen, by manipulating the election results then they should never ever abandon the White House, he should have used the United States military to restore order, just take a look how the Democrats/Judeo Bolsheviks used the military against the people and a sitting president when we will not ever have a fair and balanced election in this country again.

I will discuss the election issue in the United States in the next chapter. If you cannot have a fair and balanced election in a country, then, in that case, the form of the Republic/democracy no longer exists in a particular country like the US.

So, the next question should be, should Donald Trump run for president again?

Absolutely not, and that is because he was the weakest president. Yes, he did create a few jobs for people. Yes, he somewhat reduced the number of illegal immigrants coming to this country under his presidency. However, when the hour of triumph came, he chickened out and ran out of the White House like a rat out of a sinking ship.

Let's assume for a moment that this election was manipulated/stolen.

If he knew that the election was stolen, he should have gathered up a few hundred loyal Marines/Green Berets and he should have fought for the presidency that was stolen from him.

The next question and the real question is, can America be saved?

The answer to that particular question has two answers. The first answer is yes. However, to save America from the communist Bolshevik takeover by the communist bombs, the president cannot be a wishy-washy person. In the next election, the person who runs for president will have to have some guts and fortitude to save this nation from disaster.

The next question is why Donald Trump should not run for president. I do not know, but maybe the American people like living in the so-called toilet bowl. That is because, after one term with the current president,

America will be nothing more than a toilet bowl in itself.

Maybe Intel the American people experience the bread lines, grocery stores, and the shortages of common household goods in a store. Maybe then the American people will wake up. I pray, however, that they will wake up soon because this country lives in a desperate situation.

And the other hand, president Tromp, or Mr. Trump, does not need all this aggravation from you leftist communist bombs; he has everything he needs.

It seems that the American people are no longer interested in self-improvement and the improvement of our nation of the United States.

Suppose the American people, like the Third World nations so much and they love living in the toilet bowl that this nation will become, thanks to our bumbling politicians. In that case, that cannot make it the right decision. Well, in that case, the American people, in my opinion, deserve to drown in their own feces and the rest of their garbage. There's nothing that people like myself and many others can do about that, especially people like Mr. Donald Trump if the people of the United States of America want to turn our country the greatest country on earth by the way into a Third World toilet bowl, maybe we should let them do that all we have to do, I mean the educated class of people all we have to do is just sit back and watch what happens.

It seems to me that people in America today don't even have respect for themselves, then how can we expect them to have respect for their own country like the United States.

Every time someone puts out an idea on how to improve the conditions in our nation, from the conservative side, the leftist communist bombs, always shouted down. I wonder how much longer the nation can function like that.

Ladies and gentlemen, let's be honest in our discussion here if the United States ceases to exist as a nation, what do you think the rest of you idiots are going to do? You think that other nations will take your way and give you all the benefits or goodies that they have for their own citizens. If you think, Ladies, please think again, because other nations have stricter immigration laws than we do, I will give you an example. For example, a country like Egypt does not allow people with disabilities to apply for citizenship. All I know is what all you lefties and you communist bombs think, you're going to say that the law is racist. Well, guess what? Your opinions in Egypt do not matter, countries like Egypt, Saudi Arabia, Dubai or even Mexico are not America, and they don't have to play by your stupid rules.

For example, Mexico states in their laws that the Mexican government has the right to remove you if you present in their country is undesirable to their well-being.

Or something to that effect, all I bet you lefties and you communist bombs don't like that either, well guess what, like I said before those countries are not America and they don't have to play by you leftist rules.

You see, because those nations at least have their survival and preservation instincts intact.

I'm going to give you one other countries immigration rules, this country is called Switzerland, and for you to get residency status, not citizenship, you will have to be able to support yourself, you will have to be able to speak the language, and there is no welfare for foreigners in

Switzerland. So, in this case, all you welfare Kings and welfare Queens are just out of luck. Believe it, or not those countries such as Mexico, Switzerland and the Arab countries are watching what is going on in our country. They know that this system is unsustainable and will not allow the same BS when it comes to the country's finances.

What is really happening in America today is that all of those Third World nations in South America have opened up their jails. Also, they have opened up the mental institutions and sent all their unproductive citizens to us to the United States of America because those countries know that we are a bunch of do-gooders and, we will take any Tom Dick and Harry that the South American countries will send us, that is because they know in those countries that America has lost its survival and preservation instinct.

It does not matter the two those countries; whether those immigrants that are coming from the Third World nations will be a positive or negative influence on the United States. They just got rid of their own unproductive citizens and those countries in South America are very happy about that, and that's all, in reality, they care about.

CHAPTER 7

Replacement of the Population in the United States

As of this writing, we are experiencing and major existential crisis at our southern border of the United States.

This is happening not by chance or an accident; this is being done, by people like the New World Order crowd, people like George Soros and the rest of that ilk.

This is happening because the communist Judeo Bolsheviks want to stay in power and make the American people dependent on the government from the womb to the tomb. The question becomes, who will pay for all the free goodies that the government will give not to you, the American people? Furthermore, those other goodies will not go to the citizens of the United States. This, however, will go to the people, who came from the Third World nations, basically innovated and took away our nation's sovereignty and violated every law in the process.

If the nation does not have its own borders, its own language and its own culture, then this is not a nation not at all.

Okay, you idiots, I know what you're thinking, if this country fails all emigrate to other countries, not so fast, here are some immigration rules of other countries. Egypt here is their immigration law. For example, if you are a person with either a mental or physical disability, then the country of Egypt will not grant you residency or citizenship. What are you guys and you leftist bombs going to do about what you will do, call the president of Egypt general cc a racist? What are you going to try to put them down and complain to the United Nations? Look, you got to realize something, countries like Egypt or Mexico are not America; they do not have to play by your own leftist rules.

You see, countries like Mexico, Egypt, or Switzerland are watching us and what is going on in our country. Therefore, they're most definitely not going to allow what happened in the United States, happen to their own nation.

Mexico has a statement in their immigration will that says that you have to be useful to their society and you have to contribute to their country's well-being in a positive way.

Also, Mexico reserves the right to throw you out of their country if they find that you present in their country negatively influences their society.

Saudi Arabia has will never grant you citizenship. They will give you a two-year work visa, where you can get extended. However, after your visa expires, you will have to leave the country.

They do, by the way, force their immigration laws.

Well, some of you may say that this is inhumane. Like I said before, Saudi Arabia is not America; they don't have to worry about what you think. As a matter of fact, they don't even care what you lefties say or think about them.

You see, those countries still have some survival and preservation instincts. They will put their people's agenda first. Most of all, those countries such as Saudi Arabia and Switzerland to appoint and Egypt don't care what people think about them worldwide. I think we can definitely learn lessons from them.

If we still want to be the great power in this world, the only thing we should care about is our own and our people's well-being, not about the people that come from the garbage can countries.

The only thing useless bombs can do about those countries like Egypt and Saudi Arabia is call them racist. That is because you people have lost your argument on everything, especially on the immigration issue that I'm discussing in this particular chapter.

I personally think in our case, being selfish and caring about our country is great, because let's face it, ladies and gentlemen, where are you going to go when this country, the United States of America, collapses on itself? The answer to that question is nowhere.

Because those countries know that if you have trashed your own country, they will not let you turn their own country into the next trashcan.

Absolutely yes, those countries are very selfish and that is a very good thing because those countries have not lost their survival instinct yet and I hope they never do.

However, if we, the American people, do not get our act together, we are finished as a nation, which is the big problem. The big question is, how would we live in this post-collapse system?

Living in the post-economic collapse, hearing the United States will be very difficult for some people, that is because those people were never taught how to make do, with less and unfortunately, people have become more dependent on technology.

Those of you who came to America from Eastern Europe through the early 70s and the late 80s will know how to survive in the society that will be dominant by the leftist communist bombs. Especially when it comes to getting in line for the basic items needed for day-to-day living, that is because you guys still have what we call the basic survival instinct.

However, those of us who grew up on Xbox and many other goodies do not have the survival instinct that will be necessary to survive in the post-economic collapse of the United States.

The survival for the generation that grew up in the late 90s and early 2000 will be difficult because all of those things in our dear old public schools such as woodshop, car mechanics were taken out of our dear old public schools.

This is because the next economy after the collapse will be skills-based. It will not be, based on how many names and how many degrees you have after your name.

What's even worse about this is that your teachers and parents gave you this utopian world that does not really exist. This is because your teachers, your guidance counselors try to in high school and even college to protect you from the real world. They did not teach you how the real world works, so those of you, in that case, core brainwashed by your parents by your teachers and the whole entire American educational system, I will almost guarantee you will not survive the upcoming collapse and the post-world because you do not know. You don't have the skill set necessary for you to survive.

In this particular chapter, we talked about that people in America today lack basic survival instincts, which is true. They also lack even a basic instinct of self-preservation.

However, what I want to concentrate on in this chapter now is why the American people and the American population are being replaced?

The answer to this particular question is that the powers that be do like more obedient population, that is, the Communists and the Bolsheviks, can stay in power indefinitely and so that they can promote their unsustainable by the way, one welfare programs and other goodies.

What you have to also understand about this population replacement here in the United States is that those countries in South America are not sending their best and brightest here, what happened was they opened up their mental institutions and their jails and let those people come here to the United States and basically, turn our country into basically a toilet bowl let's come on, I know that I am being harsh here, however, if you want to, survive in this post-collapse world, you will have to get a very strong those in reality and how the real world works.

You see, those people coming from South America and other garbage can countries are going to be basically told by the Democrats and the Communists to just shut up and vote Democrat, of course, if we're going to have elections in this country anyway.

Because of the importation of the people from the Third World, the American citizen will be treated and his own country as a third-class or even fourth class citizen/human being that is because what you don't realize is that all those goodies that the Democrats want, such as the basic income or the universal basic income might not even go to the American citizen. However, this may go to the people that came here from the garbage can country.

CHAPTER 8

The Thin Blue Line

Nowadays, you hear a lot about so-called defunding police here in America. We all know who is behind this phenomenon. We don't have to look too far for the answer because behind all this circus stands you leftist communist Democrat bums, you see you cannot have a total communist takeover, Intel you destroy the following institutions, you're education institutions and your police and military institutions.

I know what you're saying that we can do without the military and other security institutions. I will answer this question in this way, most of you would not last on the street five minutes without police protection and there are many different reasons for that.

Another issue will be discussed in this chapter, which is dismantling the security apparatus from within that is also a bad idea.

Your next question should be, why are the Communists and the Bolsheviks or doing this? That is because you have to remember a couple of words that I went to tell you now, the name of the game is controlled and in order for the Bolsheviks to achieve this, they have to dismantle the most important institutions in the country, which two of them are your military and your local police.

Most of you do not understand this; that is, if they dismantle the police, the Communists will definitely replace today's police with their own Bolshevik hoodlums, and believe me, once they dismantle this police force in this military and replace it with their own it will be more brutal than the last one.

Most of you are saying all well, I could live without the police or the military, most of you don't even have the necessary skills to survive in an environment, like that, most of you sat in front of the TVs and played call of duty, which you little Xbox, believe me when the thin Blue Line falls and our society falls life is not going to be like the videogame call of duty. Most of the people in America today have become sedentary we spend too much time on our computers and other devices and in part of the TV, so I will guarantee you that if they dismantled the police and the military and other security apparatus, you would not last in this society five minutes.

We already had a sort of economic collapse that was in Iraq, when we overthrew Saddam Hussein, and then when the present Iraq Saddam Hussein, got removed from office by force, after that the streets became chaotic, in my opinion, the American people, the majority of them would not even know what to do if they found themselves in this particular situation but if the communist Bolsheviks have their way this country will turn into, another lawless nation maybe even worse than Somalia, back in the 90s, this is what can happen if the Bolsheviks and their left-wing useless idiots have their way and if they will succeed in dismantling the nation's security apparatus.

The next question is, who would want to become a police officer or work in some sort of law enforcement?

Today's law enforcement officers and the military have become nothing more than a bunch of babysitters and counselors. That is because our police officers, due to the influence of communists and Bolsheviks in our government, cannot do the job that they were tasked with.

When it comes to defunding the police, this is already happening here in America. Ladies and gentlemen, it already happened in Portland,

Oregon. In that particular state, neighborhoods have become basically ghost towns and that is, putting it mildly. When the defunding of the police really take effect, you have to understand that those policemen are not going to protect you. All they are going to care about is their own families, by the way, justifiably so.

I basically feel that you can certainly, warn the American people but tell those people who experience the hostility and chaos. In my opinion, they do not know what they're talking about.

I will guarantee you that if they really dismantle the police because of defunding the police by the communist left and the Bolsheviks, you will be screaming. Please bring the police back when this chaos gets underway shortly, in case it will be too late.

You know you can certainly talk big about defunding the police and dismantling the law enforcement and our security apparatus, but because none of you have the necessary skills to survive in a chaotic situation. Like that, you will be the first to yell, police, please help us; however, when the communist Bolsheviks take over, it will be too late.

We can definitely not do anything about this type of behavior because, in that case, people will have to learn from their mistakes. However, in this case, I do not think people will not learn anything from their mistakes that are because they are not aware of what is really going on behind the scenes during this so-called fund the police movement that is sponsored by the so-called Judeo Bolsheviks.

There is a saying beware of what you wish for, that is because, in reality, I will guarantee you that this will not have a very good outcome, because of the defunding of the police, a lot of innocent people will suffer, this will not be the utopian society that the Judeo Bolsheviks are trying to sell you.

The people who will suffer during this coming crisis will be the average middle-class American citizen, and there is nothing that you will be able to do when the Bolsheviks themselves will implement this program of defunding the police.

There is another scenario that had already happened, about the dismantling of the police, yes dismantling of the police scenario already happened in 1939, on September 17.

We all remember that World War II started on September 1, 1939, in Poland when Germany invaded it but what you have to remember is in 1939 when the Germans invaded Poland on September 1, because of the pack that Germany saw a signed with the Soviet Union, the Soviet army also innovated the other half of Poland, towards the East on September 17, on that day some cities in the East were defended such as Grodno, Vilo and Luwuw, you see in those cities when the Soviets and you communist Bolsheviks took over, they immediately this man told and hunted down the city officials, such as the city mayors and other city officials this also meant, the Polish police and security apparatus and replaced it with their own Bolshevik communist police, known as the NKVD, this police force was part of the main Communist Party of the Soviet Union, and they answer to Joseph Stalin the leader of the Soviet Union directly.

Because of these orders from Joseph Stalin, when the Soviet Union took over Poland's cities to the East, they liquidated all the educated people, including professors, primary school teachers, doctors, and policeman polish policemen, who did not agree with the Soviet Union dictatorship.

I know that some of you may not remember and maybe not know about the NKVD massacre of Polish intellectuals and military leaders in the Katyni forest.

I know what you're saying that, when the Bolsheviks implement their dismantling of the police and the security apparatus here in America, they will not do that.

I hope not. However, what they might do is they may use other repressive tactics and they will definitely replace this particular police force and other security apparatuses with their own version of the NKVD.

So before you say let's bring the system down and dismantle the police, I think you should learn from history, so you don't repeat the same mistakes.

CHAPTER 9

The Incompetence of the American Senior Citizen

Most of you who have read my books obviously know by now that I have been very harsh on the baby boomer and older generations.

However, have you ever asked yourself why?

I have been harsh on the senior citizens and the baby boomer generation because when Richard E Nixon took us off the gold standard, there weren't any protests, or nobody mentioned it back.

Well, guess what? I will be even harsher on the baby boomer and the older generation in this chapter.

When Congress passed the Obama Care bill, the older generation again failed to speak out against it. The Obama Care bill is a dangerous law to any older person in America today because basically, it dictates to the doctor what the doctor can do for you when you reach the ripe old age of 65 – 75.

Lots of people said that Donald Trump has gotten rid of Obama Care. This is further from the truth that you will ever know, that is because, yes, Donald J. Trump, the 45th President of the United States, has gotten rid of the mandate that you have to buy Obama Care so-called medical insurance. However, what you do not understand is that all the other provisions are still in the bill. One of them is the so-called death panel. What is that mean, you may ask?

This actually means that when you reach your so-called golden years, you will not get the medical care that you need. Let me explain it a little bit further. Say, for example, you may need a heart transplant to live longer. Well, in that case, if you reach the old age of 60 to 75, that means you will not be eligible for that particular heart transplant, because you are, as they say to old, you see before the Obama Care bill went into, in fact, you probably could get the transplant, however because of this bill right now if her senior citizen you are basically out of luck. You are the older generation, always taught us to be good stewards and if something is wrong with the system, we should speak out. However, when the new Obama bill called the Obama Care has passed, none of you from the older generation even raised a peek about that.

I know sometimes your baby boomers you, accuse us of being disrespected, to the older generation, well how can we respect you guys, if you do not have respect for yourselves, respect for yourselves especially when the United States government through the Obama Care medical bill, dictates to you yes I'm talking to you baby boomers and the older generation when the government decides how long is a person going to live this does not sit well with me and if you have any respect for yourselves then they should definitely bother you because it starts with you the older generation then it moves on to the people with disabilities, and many other things.

Yes, I may speak out about this issue because once you take a walk and open this Pandora's box, who knows where this issue will end up. I do not know but, maybe you older generation loves this so-called New World Order, but guess what I do not want any part of it, especially when they pass laws that will determine how long a person lives. I know that you taught us about respect for life. However, how can you still teach us about that when our dear government is basically keeping the most or communion part of the Obama Care bill, where it will definitely affect us, in ways that we still don't even know, okay let me give you another scenario, what if somebody is born with a disability, then what over the to put him on so-called death panel that is included in the Obama Care bill.

When you get it when we get into the discussion of Obama Care and its consequences, we truly are opening what we call a can of worms because you see in actuality, the New World Order is testing us on how far they're going to push the process of population control by euthanasia.

However, since our dear old senior citizens didn't even bother to examine and read the bill after it passed, since none of the old senior citizens or seasoned citizens did not even have the guts to come out and protest the new Obama Care bill then, we do have most certainly a problem.

In which case I have to say that yes, Donald J. Trump, the 45th president of the United States he got rid of, the so-called insurance mandate, which means that you do not have to have Obama Care as your primary medical insurance, however because of all the poison pills in that particular bill, the other male the other measures of the Obama Care bill, stayed in place, that includes the death panels.

You see, in this case, and I know what I'm going to say, it will be very controversial here. Our dear old, senior citizens signed their own death warrant by not speaking out and not studying how actually the Obama Care bill actually works. You always told us that we should have respect for elders, and that is, May I say, a good idea, but how can we have respect for elders if our elders don't even have respect for yourselves.

Don't you understand that the New World Order and their game is all about control? However, when we are talking about the Obama Health

Care bill, we are talking about actual population control itself.

Now those of you, senior citizens who want to live longer, unfortunately, because of this Obama Health Care bill you will have to go to our hospital, outside of the United States and guess what, those countries do not take such things like your old Medicare, like your insurance, so in which case you will have to pay, out-of-pocket for you treatment that you will need that is because of this Obama Care bill, some of the treatment that is necessary for your health will not be given to you here in the United States.

The only people you can thank for this is you freeloaders who think that Obama Care itself it's free, not that is a lot of hogwash, that is because when it comes to your health and other things in this country, it is not free that is because whether we want to or not, sooner or later you will end up paying for things one way or the other.

Your older generation has taught us to think before we act, well, in this case, I'm going to give you a new phrase to memorize or think before you vote so that such absurd like the Obama Care bill does not happen again, because remember this it is easy, to pass the law, however, if the law does not work it is very hard to repeal it later on.

CHAPTER 10

The Existence of a Nation

In America, many people on the left and right political spectrum say that certain country has a right to exist. Well, I'm afraid I have to disagree with the people on the left and on the right of the political spectrum in this case. I thought about this for a very long time, and I concluded that no country has a right to exist.

The only reason that countries do exist is that some of them have the natural instinct of self-preservation and survival, whether through their strong economic, military and intellectual fortitude.

Let me give you an example, if a certain country cannot sustain itself economically, intellectually or militarily sooner or later, this country will be swept away by the sense of time.

Okay, you liberals, if every country has a right to exist, why don't we bring back the ancient city of Pompeii, or even what are we bring back, the ancient city of Cartage.

Of course, you liberals will say that the lava covered up the ancient city of Pompeii from the mouth of Vesuvius. You guys are not wrong in this case. However, have you ever bothered to ask yourself why the ancient Romans did not bother to rebuild the city of Pompeii after the Volcano Vesuvius interruption?

I will answer this particular question because it was too expensive for the ancient Romans to rebuild this particular city. This also brings me back to the liberal left argument that the state of Israel has the right to exist. Like I said before, no country has a right to exist. We have supported the state of Israel for about 50 years, give or take a decade. If a country cannot survive on its own after all these years, then there is something wrong with this picture.

All by the way, if we're added if we can make the argument that every country has a right to exist, then why do we bring back the ancient civilization of Egypt, for example, or even one way bring back the ancient city of Atlantis.

In reality, all empires are born, they rise, they reach a certain pinnacle, and they fall; that is the natural progression of things. Believe it or not, America is an empire to and because of its economic, moral to some degree, military and intellectual decline, America will end up just like those ancient civilizations that I have mentioned above.

Those of you who have read my previous books will know why this is happening right now. Yes, every country in the world is experiencing its downturn now, especially a country like America.

You might be asking the next question, can we, the American people survive the decline of America itself as a country? The answer to that question is absolutely yes. However, there are things that people will have to change about themselves. One thing you guys can do is to change your priorities.

The second thing you can definitely do is to learn how to live within your means. The third thing you will have to do is restore your primary and secondary survival and preservation instinct. To do this, you will have to sit down and really think about what are things that are important to you.

Let's take this discussion a little bit farther down the road. We all know that all those civilizations such as Egypt cartage and many others have experienced some sort of economic collapse, or we may speculate and say that those particular ancient civilizations have also experienced all three things such as moral military weakness and economic weakness, all of those things have contributed to the fall of those ancient civilizations.

America is no different from ancient Rome; if we are going to look at it from this point of view. Yes, America is an empire. There's nothing wrong with that; however, you have to understand that all empires have beginning and ending cycles, just like everything else on this planet.

So if next time the liberal left or the extreme right says that the country of Israel has a right to exist, they have not well studied the rise and fall of the ancient civilizations.

So if they're going to start to argue for or against this so-called theory, I think they should look at the history that is because, let's face it, sometimes history has a way of repeating itself.

We can even look at the ancient civilization of Mesopotamia, which is the modern-day country of Iraq. Those people had a very thriving ancient civilization. However, because of maybe their economic decline, that particular civilization has fallen as well.

So, in this case, if the liberal left or the extreme right says to you that countries have a right to exist, I do not think they understand what they're talking about in the first place. It is only natural that are civilizations rise and fall, and in my opinion, if people interfere in this particular natural cycle, then at the end of the day, they will be their own victims.

After careful analysis of certain issues, I concluded that after the US economic collapse, this country would turn into hopefully tribalism, mind you that whether this country totally seizes to exist or turns into one and of tribes, if you are not sufficiently prepared for this, whether mentally physically or spiritually you will definitely have a hard time, surviving and living in that type of environment, you'll be lucky we will be lucky, if this country does turn into tribalism, that is because if this country the United States totally seizes to exist as a nation then we will be in big trouble.

Your next question should be, why is it better if this country turns into tribalism, then totally seizing to exist? The answer to that particular question is very simple, because in that case, if this nation turns into some sort of tribalism, then we as human beings have a chance to survive and believe me, it is not going to be like Mad Max or the Red Dawn movie, however, if your have and you can keep your wits about you, then you will survive and probably make it in this post-apocalyptic world. Those people, in my opinion, who do not learn from their history turn to repeat the mistakes they have made.

Whether we look at places like Ancient Rome, the Ancient City of Atlantis, or the Ancient Egyptian civilization, several factors lead to those nations' collapse. In our case, history is repeating itself all over again.

That is why you need to read this particular book to make and take the necessary steps so that you can survive the things that are going to happen here in the United States.

ABOUT THE AUTHOR

Mark Wrobel resides in Wilmington, Delaware, and was born with a disability. But it didn't allow that to stop him from excelling in life. His father raised Mark; he was a dedicated single parent. He grew up in a communist system. Due to his disability, his country would not allow him to attend school with regular kids, but he persevered. Fortunately, when he was about 10 years old, he came to the United States, which he knew was the land of opportunity. So, he took full advantage of it and made sure he got a good education.

From 1989 until 1993, he attended St. Thomas The Apostle School, a Catholic school in Wilmington, Delaware.

Then in 1993, he attended Wilmington High School and graduated in 1997 with a high school diploma.

In 2002, Mark attended Delaware Tech Community College to attend their Web Designer Certificate Program, which he completed.

He continued his education in 2008 at Strayer University, studying Information Systems and Homeland Security. Mark graduated from Stayer in 2012 with an Associate Degree.

In 2018, he returned to Strayer University to obtain his Bachelor of

Science Degree in Information Systems and Homeland Security Management and graduated in 2020. He is proud of this accomplishment because he was told that it was impossible and he couldn't do it.

Mark is currently employed with the United States Coast Guards in Communications. He began working for the Coast Guard in 2012. Thus far, he has received multiple awards and accolades for his dedicated service. Mark loves to learn and try new things.

In 2007, he decided to try sky diving and with the help of an instructor, he jumped 18,000 feet. There was an article published about it in the News Journal.

In the future, he would like to go back to school to obtain his master's and a doctoral degree.

Mark is the author of the titles Start of the Coming Civil War, Progressive Credentialism Versus Ageism, The American Holocaust, Unknown Secrets of World War II, which are available online worldwide. The Fall of the American Empire is his fifth book and he couldn't have done it without his father's support.

REFERENCES

Richard Nixon got us off the gold standard.
https://www.foxnews.com/opinion/forty-years-ago-today-nixon-took-us-off-the-gold-standard

the definition of inflation or hyperinflation
https://www.investopedia.com/terms/h/hyperinflation.asp#:~:text=Hyperinflation%20is%20a%20term%20to%20describe%20rapid%2C%20excessive%2C,inflation%2C%20typically%20measuring%20more%20than%2050%25%20per%20month.

Printing of money
(https://www.investopedia.com/terms/q/quantitative-easing.asp, 2020)

The fall of Afghanistan https://radio.foxnews.com/2021/09/27/a-look-at-taliban-rule-from-inside-kabul/

https://radio.foxnews.com/2021/08/21/from-washington-what-does-the-fall-of-afghanistan-mean-for-the-upcoming-9-11-anniversary/

The fall of the Soviet Union 1989 – 1991
https://www.globalsecurity.org/military/world/russia/soviet-collapse.htm#:~:text=Collapse%20of%20the%20Soviet%20Union%20-%201989-1991%20The,the%20resources%20of%20more%20than%20a%20dozen%20countries.

China is teaching martial arts in school https://www.gooverseas.com/study-abroad/china/academic explorers/15788

https://www.reddit.com/r/martialarts/comments/2t1fpe/are_martial_arts_more_commonly_taught_in_asian/

information technology and the Middle Easthttps://www.e-ir.info/2019/05/23/science-technology-and-security-in-the-middle-east/

transgender will be allowed to serve in the military and the US

transgender personnel serving in the US militaryhttps://www.therainbowtimesmass.com/transgender-bipartisan-bill-allow-transgender-people-serve-military/

https://www.foxnews.com/us/us-military-lifts-ban-on-transgenders-serving-openly

massacre of Polish officershttps://en.wikipedia.org/wiki/Katyn_massacre

prostitution in Syrian refugee camps

https://www.timesofisrael.com/in-jordan-desperate-syrian-refugees-turn-to-prostitution/situation at the US-Mexico borderhttps://www.foxnews.com/politics/tens-thousands-migrants-southern-border-remain-in-mexico-restart

the Bolsheviks take over the American schoolshttps://www.foxnews.com/us/oregon-teacher-american-flag-classroom-violence-menace-intolerance

there is no gold in Fort Knoxhttps://www.bing.com/videos/search?q=No+gold+in+Fort+Knox+the+history+Channel&docid=608029689783724020&mid=878AA2BAB0C4FE59B145878AA2BAB0C4FE59B145&view=detail&FORM=VIRE

Egyptian immigration and naturalization processhttps://en.wikipedia.org/wiki/Egyptian_nationality_law

Switzerland citizenship law https://studyinginswitzerland.com/immigration-switzerland-laws-requirements/

Saudi Arabia citizenship law https://www.justlanded.com/english/Saudi-Arabia/Saudi-Arabia-Guide/Visas-Permits/Citizenship

Obama Care that panels https://www.foxnews.com/politics/death-panel

the next caravan at the US-Mexico border https://www.borderreport.com/hot-topics/immigration/new-haitian-caravan-heading-for-u-s-border-in-20-days-activist-says/

the ancient city of Pompeii https://en.wikipedia.org/wiki/Pompeii

the ancient civilization of Egypt https://www.khanacademy.org/humanities/world-history/world-history-beginnings/ancient-egypt-hittites/a/egypt-article

the ancient city of Cartage https://en.wikipedia.org/wiki/Ancient_Carthage

the ancient city of Atlantis https://www.worldatlas.com/articles/the-lost-city-of-atlantis.html

Mark live in explained Mexico immigration rules https://www.youtube.com/watch?v=D5cDcI-o8cM

the former head of the ballon unit speaks about or foreign policy and the countries right to exist.

https://www.youtube.com/watch?v=XEQviZPyeXk

https://www.bing.com/videos/search?q=The+head+of+the+CIA+bin+Laden+unit%2c+speaks+out+about+the+countries+right+to+exist&&view=detail&mid=7CBAFD34D4DE21F8759F7CBAFD34D4DE21F8759F

&&FORM=VRDGAR&ru=%2Fvideos%2Fsearch%3Fq%3DThe%2520head%2520of%2520the%2520CIA%2520bin%2520Laden%2520unit%252C%2520speaks%2520out%2520about%2520the%2520countries%2520right%2520to%2520exist%26qs%3DHS%26form%3DQBVDMH%26sp%3D1%26sc%3D6-0%26cvid%3DC55272E96CFC433080C3DD177FCC9846

www.ingramcontent.com/pod-product-compliance
Lightning Source LLC
LaVergne TN
LVHW020440080526
838202LV00055B/5277